HOW SWEET IT IS

The 1966 Elston Red Devils

Matthew A. Werner

ISBN: 978-0692303801

Cover designed by James Robertson
www.jamesro.com

To the people of Michigan City,

Would you believe?
How sweet it is!
Hey, hey, all the way!

Contents

How Sweet It Is

FOUR GUYS WALK INTO A ROOM

Four men, ages sixty-six to sixty-eight, recently gathered in a meeting room. Thinning hair, graying hair. They greeted each other with a "Hey," or a "How's it going." Not as a question, but a statement. Nobody shook hands. They were comfortable. At ease. Smiling. Three of them anyway.

"Wouldn't you know Rob would get in trouble as soon as he walked into the building."

"Who tries to take coffee into a library?"

"How was I supposed to know?"

"It's always you, Rob. You're always the one to get into trouble." Jim laughed hard. They all laughed. They couldn't help it. That joke is fifty years old.

Rob rolled his head, "My god, I'm just the one who always gets caught."

"Can't take you anywhere."

There is good-natured ribbing.

"You don't look too bad."

Talk of people they knew.

"You heard Barb passed away recently."

"No, really? Man, when did that happen?"

Most of all, there was laughter. Real laughter. Deep, meaningful laughter. My God, there was a lot of laughter.

Terry Morse, O'Neil Simmons, Jim Cadwell, and Rob McFarland. Four seniors on the 1966 Indiana state basketball championship team. We talked about basketball, Elston High School, Red Devil pride, and Coach Doug Adams.

I'd already talked to their assistant coach, Al Whitlow, and their principal, Warren Jones, I said. Morse volunteered to get the guys together. A Saturday. "We'd probably like to meet in the late morning," he said, "then we'll go somewhere to eat afterward. Preferably a place that serves beer."

I knew then I was going to like these guys.

Basketball has long been king in Indiana and in 1966 Michigan City Elston was the potentate of the Hoosier state. Bill Redfield, long-time Michigan City sports editor, once summarized that season in two sentences:

> This may have been the year of the horse in China, but it was the year of the Red Devils in Indiana.
>
> The Red Devils—the Michigan City High variety—went from crippling early season injuries to glory before nearly 15,000 fans and untold radio and television audiences Saturday night, March 19, in Indianapolis.

That was it in a nutshell. Everyone who has lived in Michigan City over the last fifty years has heard of the 1966 team. I grew up years later on a farm in Union Mills, Indiana, and I'd heard of them. Mythologized over the years. They were legends, I was told.

The team won twenty-six games and lost three. Their average margin of victory was twenty-one points. More than 12,000 people turned out for the victory rally at Ames Field after the team won State. Life-sized cutouts of each player hang on a wall inside Michigan City High School. Decades before that, they clung to a wall high above the basketball court in Elston's Red Devil Gym. But those are trivial facts and leftover mementos. There is more to the story. Much more. Parts of the story nobody has told. And it all started with an unlikely coach who took an unwanted job.

AN UNLIKELY BASKETBALL COACH

A 1943 graduate of Hammond High School, Doug Adams served two years in the Army during World War II and then attended Ball State University where he played football. Upon graduation, he took his first teaching job at Riley grade school in Michigan City in 1949.

Adams wanted to coach football, but there were no open positions when he arrived. However, the assistant basketball and Junior Varsity (JV) coaching position was open. Adams later said, "nobody else wanted the job," so he took it. And why not? If for no other reason, it got his foot in the door of the high school athletic department and brought in a little extra income for Doug, his wife, Betty, their two-year-old daughter, Michele, and one-year-old son, Mike.

In his second year, an assistant football coach positon opened and Adams jumped at the chance. Every fall he assisted the football team and every winter he assisted the basketball team.

For eight years, Adams coached the Pink Imps, as the JV basketball team was known then, and worked under head coaches Dee Kohlmeier, Ick Osborne, and Ralph Hooker. When Adams got the chance to take over as head coach in 1957, the job provided a nice pay raise and Elston's basketball team was synonymous with winning. It had strung together five straight winning seasons—including three twenty-win seasons—and seven straight Sectional championships. Principal Warren Jones was glad to see Adams get promoted. "Doug Adams was a good coach and a good man," he said. "He was a good leader of young men. He set a good example."

But Adams first season got off to a rocky start. "We had four losses by Christmas and I'm sure that everyone began wondering if they had hired the right man for the job," Adams once said in an interview with Dennis Edgington, author of the book, *Hey, We're Red Devils*. The team also lost the first game in its own holiday tournament that season. Things looked grim. If Adams wanted to keep his job, he would need to win more games.

Warren Jones and I sat at his kitchen table talking about basketball, Elston High School, and Coach Doug Adams. "Doug was a good football player at Ball State. He never played a game of basketball in his life. Never. Not in high school or college," said Jones.

Wait. What? He told you that?

"Yeah."

I'm guessing he didn't tell many people that.

Jones grinned. "No, probably not, but I knew it. But I didn't publish it."

Not only did Doug Adams never play a game of basketball, "He never dribbled a basketball in his whole *life*," said his son, Mike.

Make no mistake about it, Adams wanted to coach football and he continued to do so after taking charge of the basketball program. In the fall of 1957, '58, '59, '60, '61, he continued to work with the football team and teach the boys the finer points of the game. in the autumn of 1962, he focused his energy on basketball and left football for good. But he did coach the cross country team and pushed his basketball players to join in order to get in shape for the upcoming season.

Looking back, if townspeople had known that Adams never played a lick of basketball, they might have run him out of town before New Year's Day 1958 when his first team didn't look so great. Good thing for the boys who played for Coach Adams, his secret was safe. Good thing for Michigan City, Indiana, too.

After that disappointing 4-4 start, Adams managed to turn his team around in a big way. The Red Devils won the next sixteen games in a row before losing by two points to East Chicago Washington in the first round of the Regional.

Ah, yes—East Chicago Washington and the dreaded Regional jinx! Despite the team's success, one obstacle seemed insurmountable: a Regional championship. For decades, the winner of the LaPorte County Sectional advanced to the "meat grinder" Calumet Regional held in Hammond and later, East Chicago. Year in and year out, the state's top-ranked teams fought to win that Regional and advance onto the Semi-state tournament. Since 1924, Elston had won just two Regionals and its last championship occurred in 1935.

East Chicago Washington foiled Michigan City's efforts to take home the Regional crown again in 1959, 1962, and 1963. Gary Roosevelt spurned the Red Devils in 1960 and 1961. In 1964, Gary Tolleston defeated Michigan City in the Regional.

Fans wanted their team to win, but they had grown to believe the Regional was beyond their grasp. It wasn't meant to be. Their school had been hexed. But Adams had a different feeling about it as he explained to Dennis Edgington years later.

> It wasn't driving me as crazy as it was the townspeople, because they were seeing a jinx. What I saw were superior ballclubs. They were great basketball teams. Looking back, there isn't one time I could say we didn't give it our all.
>
> During that time, Washington was riding the crest of their greatest teams, and it didn't matter who came out of Gary, one of them was going to be outstanding. If it wasn't Roosevelt, then Froebel or Tolleston would slip in there.
>
> It's sad that most people only remember that you lost. We were involved in some of the greatest games and come-backs that Regional ever saw. I can't remember going in there the favorite too many times.

MAYBE NEXT YEAR

By the mid-Sixties, schools across Indiana were consolidating at a rapid pace. The LaPorte County Sectional tournament had sixteen teams in the 1950s, but had dropped to twelve teams in 1964 and then ten teams in 1965.

The Indiana High School Athletic Association (IHSAA) allowed the number of schools participating in individual Sectional tournaments to vary, but it maintained sixty-four Sectional sites and sixteen Regionals with four teams per Regional. Scrambling to keep up with the rapid decrease in the number of high schools, tournaments were constantly being reorganized and teams shifted to different Sectional and Regional sites to keep things balanced.

In 1965, the Elston Red Devils won the Sectional for the fourteenth straight time, but that year the team didn't travel to the meat grinder in East Chicago. Instead, the IHSAA sent the winner east to the Elkhart Regional. Elston went 15-5 in the regular season and was co-champions of the Northern Indiana Conference. Many fans were optimistic about the change of venue and thought maybe this was the year. The newspaper headline read, "Red Devils Ready to Break Net Hex," and Bill Redfield observed that the attitude from head coach Doug Adams all the way down to the students managers believed that was the year the team would "break their regional high school basketball tournament hex." Many believed, or hoped, that going east would change Michigan City's fortunes.

Elston's first-round opponent, South Bend Washington, was the only Northern Indiana Conference team to beat them. But fans remained optimistic as everyone—including South Bend Washington coach Subby Nowicki—believed Washington had played its finest game of the season against the Red Devils on its home court a few weeks earlier. Also, several Red Devil players had been wracked with the flu at the time. Furthermore, South Bend Washington was playing in its first Regional since 1938, whereas it had become a familiar routine for Michigan City.

After tying the game, 51 – 51, one Red Devil player missed the front end of a one-and-one free throw. No problem. Then another player did the same thing.

Hmm.

The next thing fans knew, the team couldn't seem to buy a basket. After the game, LaPorte assistant superintendent Bob Miller commented that, "The ball just wouldn't go in."

With eleven seconds to go, the scoreboard read, 65 – 55, in favor of South Bend Washington. Doug Adams turned and faced his boys on the bench. Blank faces stared across the court, while the senior boys buried their faces in towels.

Bill Redfield wrote these sobering words in his "Following' Thru" column: "The Red Devils have failed 14 times in a row in the regional but on the trip home they were not disheartened. Just having played for the Red Devils satisfied a number of them."

The following Monday, a brief editorial appeared in the *News-Dispatch*.

> The Elkhart regional tournament on Saturday was
> no more productive for the Red Devils than all

those meets they attended through the years in the Calumet area, so they join other defeated Indiana high school basketball teams in hanging up suits for the season.

Some fans had built high hopes this year of cracking what has come to be known for the Red Devils as 'the regional jinx.' For them, Saturday's loss to South Bend Washington was a particularly bitter pill to swallow.

There's one compensation about athletics: Seasons come and go, and there's always another one ahead to enliven hopes.

Maybe next year will be the one for the Red Devils. . . ."

RED DEVIL PRIDE

By the start of the 1965-66 school year, baby boomers pushed attendance numbers beyond school building limits. Elston's attendance swelled from 801 students in 1950 to 1,530 in 1960 and 2,285 students in the fall of 1965 (grades ten through twelve).

Desks were squeezed into crowded classrooms. Students shuffled through congested hallways. Every student shared a locker. The school added one minute to the passing period between classes to accommodate the bottlenecks that ensued in every doorway and crosswalk. Stairways were designated one-way only to facilitate the stream of student bodies.

"If a student tried to go the wrong way up a one-way stairwell, they were going to have a rough go of it," Warren Jones laughed.

Charged with maintaining order over all of these students was the biggest Red Devil cheerleader of all: Principal Warren Jones. He worked as school principal in the 1960s, '70s, and early '80s. He strove to be aware of everything that was going on in the school. He maintained discipline and worked hard to be fair, but above everything else, "I also wanted the kids to have some fun when they were in school," Jones said.

"He was strict, but everybody liked him," said Elston junior Dave Milcarek. "He seemed to know everybody. He'd say, 'Hey Dave,' or whatever—that many kids."

Yes, all those kids! While graduating seniors couldn't identify most of the students who streamed across the stage during commencement exercises, Jones managed to know nearly every one of them.

"Really, that was my goal," Jones explained. "I liked to call the kids by their first name and I did as much as I could. I had a professor at Ball State, the first day of class, he took all of our names and the second day he called us by our first name. I was impressed, so when I started teaching, I did the same thing. I thought that was important. People like to be called by their first name."

The population boom brought new students, more diverse students, and a greater pool of athletic talent. This was a tremendous boost to building and maintaining top athletic teams, but Michigan City wasn't alone. Schools everywhere had exploded with students and new talent. To maintain an edge, Doug Adams developed a system.

As head coach, Adams hand-picked every one of the basketball coaches in the school system. He chose men he could trust. Men who knew and loved the game of basketball. Men of integrity. Men like Al Whitlow, who had played under Adams when he was the Pink Imps coach. After he earned his college degree, Whitlow became a teacher at Barker Junior High in 1961 and Adams immediately asked him to be one of his coaches.

You cannot discuss Coach Doug Adams, or his system, without talking about his long-time assistant coach, Al Whitlow.

"We had a very good working relationship," Whitlow said. "I never wanted his job. A lot of times guys want to be head coaches. I never wanted to be a head coach. That truly was not anything I wanted. So that wasn't a problem. We got along fine."

There was no doubt who was in charge—Adams was in charge. But he surrounded himself with good people for a reason.

"He listened," Whitlow said. "He had his way of doing things, but he would tell me all the time on the bench, 'Keep talking to me, keep talking to me, you know, I may not do it, or it may not catch on right away with me, but you keep talking to me.' There were times when he said, 'No, we're not going to do that.' But then there were other times where he would make changes."

No question, they made a great team. Years later in an interview, Doug Adams acknowledged that fact:

> I've never worked better with anyone as I did with Al Whitlow. He was a great thinker on his feet; still is. Many times there is tension on the bench and Al might say something and I would snap at him.
>
> He wouldn't care. 'OK, you don't like that, what about this; how about that...' He could keep firing them out until something jelled with mine, and that's what we'd do. Al didn't have one envious bone in his body and I'll always have the greatest respect and admiration for him.

Every year, Adams held a meeting of all of the coaches at all of the levels. He told them what he wanted the boys to work on, what skills needed to be developed, what fundamentals would be taught, and what offense to run. "I tell you, anybody who went through Elston and played basketball in Michigan City during that era, to this day, you put them on the floor and they'd run the box weave," Al Whitlow said. "They'd *know* how to run the box weave."

He also told the coaches what they could not do. "Like play zone defense," Whitlow recalled. "You're not going to play a zone defense, you were going to learn to play man-to-man."

Adams even instructed coaches on what skills individual players needed to develop and what positions some of the boys would play. "When Jim Cadwell was in junior high school at Barker," Whitlow said, "Doug had me have him play guard because he wanted some taller guards. Cadwell was probably 6'1". So, he played a lot of guard for us at the time."

The boys who played basketball at the elementary level and junior high level were given a basketball for the summer. When school started in the fall, the ball had to be returned and it better had been used. One year, Adams handed out goals for kids to attach to their garages at home. Another year, they received iron rings that sat inside those goals and made it smaller and harder to make a basket in an effort to turn the boys into sharp shooters.

Adams preached a 2-2-1 press defense and balanced scoring. "When you talk about Doug Adams' philosophy, it was have a balanced attack," Whitlow said. "You didn't necessarily want to have one go-to guy. You wanted to be able to attack from different angles. You wanted to have as many kids get into double figures as you could get into double figures. A balanced attack: that was definitely his philosophy."

Adams' system extended beyond fundamentals and X's and O's. He admired UCLA coach John Wooden's philosophies on basketball and life and read everything Wooden wrote. He was fair. He maintained discipline and taught the boys to do what they were supposed to do every time. He was honest and established trust. He inspired his players and wanted them to develop into fine young men. He insisted players keep good grades.

"He had to stay on me," said O'Neil Simmons. "I was an average student, 'C,' but I could have been better." Adams prodded him to do better, to realize his full potential. When Simmons went to college, he did do better and earned higher grades. If a player wanted to further his education, Adams helped him do that. If he needed a scholarship, Adams called university coaches to make that possible.

Adams' discipline was simple: if you're not going to do what you're supposed to do; you run. Up-and-overs, he called them. You ran up a walkway to the top of the gym and then back down to the floor. Then go to the next stairway. Up to the concourse, over, and back down to the floor. Up and over, up and over until you'd bounded up and down every walkway in the gymnasium.

"You can always make a mistake one time. That's a mistake," said Mike Adams. "Second time, it's your fault. There won't be a third time. The lesson: learn from your mistakes. That's what he wanted."

Terry Morse said, "We scrimmaged the Pink Imps every Wednesday night. Jim and I had three consecutive times down the court. We screwed up and threw the ball out of the way or threw it out of your hands and after the third time, we didn't even look at Coach Adams. We knew. He was pointing his finger, but we didn't even look. We just started doing up-and-overs. He cracked up laughing. We knew. It didn't matter who you were."

Adams devoted himself to basketball and teaching. He developed boys into men. He put together a booklet on how to be an Elston Red Devil. It explained how to practice. It stated that players were expected to shoot twenty-five free throws a day. They needed to learn to shoot a left-handed layup and dribble with the left hand. Also, be honest and helpful. He knew some players could not afford a coat and tie, but wear a sweater—dress respectfully when traveling as a team. Respect others. Take pride in your team and your school.

What did it mean to be a Red Devil?

"Honor," said Simmons. "At that young age, you know, if you ever went to a Red Devil game and saw the crowd and the enthusiasm—hey, you wanted to be a Red Devil."

"All the games were on the radio and when you were a kid, you would listen to the games on the radio and sit in your room and shoot a wadded paper through a little hoop. You kept score, had everybody's stats," Rob McFarland said.

"It was an amazing—I don't know about the rest of these guys, but—it was an amazing time. It really was fantastic," Jim Cadwell said.

"When we were in ninth grade—that game we played at Barker and we played Elston Junior High—the place was full. It was *full of people*. We had never seen it full before. Doug Adams happened to be there and we thought, 'Oh, geez, Doug Adams is here,'" Morse said.

Even running a dust mop across the Red Devil Gym's floor was considered a special honor. A sign that you had the inside track. That Doug Adams was watching you. That he liked what you were doing.

"When they had Sectionals, if Doug Adams would come and say, 'You get to sweep the floor,' and if you got to sweep the floor, you knew," McFarland said with a nod.

Adams pursued good sportsmanship. "Even after a loss, go shake their hands," said Mike Adams. "Tell *them* they did a great job. You're *not* going to be a sore loser."

Doug Adams was super organized and maintained a steady schedule. Sunday, he sat down and started working on the upcoming weekend's game plan. Looked at film and reviewed the scouting report. During the week, he ran practice.

Monday night, the boys worked on Fundamentals. "Every Monday night. Get the gloves out. Not grippy gloves—cotton gloves—and once you took those gloves off, that ball felt like you could feel every lump in the thing," Cadwell said.

Tuesday was offense, defense, and a rebounding drill known as Brutal Ball. For Brutal Ball, Adams put a rim shrinker on the basket and then the boys would shoot. It was no-holds-barred, anything goes. It started out three-on-three. After grabbing a rebound, the boys passed it to an outlet man. When that became too easy, they played four-on-three. Next, Adams designated guards O'Neil Simmons and Larry Gipson to be his "dogs." As soon as a boy rebounded the ball, the dogs jumped in and slapped at it, trying to knock it away. When they mastered that, Adams added a fifth boy to challenge his rebounders. Three boys trying to outrebound five with the dogs pawing at them.

The boys scraped, clawed, and fought for the rebound. They threw elbows, shoulders, hips and knees in a desperate attempt to get the ball, secure the ball, clear the ball.

Don't let the opponent get it. Gotta be tough. Keep 'em on your backs.

"Coach Adams used to say, 'I don't care what you get—bring me a head. If it's not a ball, it's a head,'" Cadwell laughed.

It was effective. Only three teams out-rebounded the Red Devils all season and those were by narrow margins.

Wednesday, the varsity scrimmaged against the Pink Imps. Practices typically lasted two hours, but scrimmage night could be short or long.

"It could go on until 9 o'clock. If you weren't playing well, he let you know," Cadwell said.

By the end of the season the goal was to keep the Pink Imps from scoring. "There was not a bunch of tin cans out there, either," Rob McFarland said. The Pink Imps were a talented group of players in their own right. The varsity took it to them as if it were a regular game. Sometimes, they would hold the Pink Imps scoreless for a full thirty minutes and Coach Adams would be pleased. Other times, they played into the late hours.

Thursday practice included the final game plan preparations as Adams prepared them for that weekend's opponents. Friday and Saturday the team executed those plans on the court against opposing teams.

He ran practices using a set of 3x5 index cards outlining what the team would do and when. Everything was regimented and planned out.

3:05 p.m, calisthenics.

3:15 p.m, up-and-overs.

3:20 p.m, ball handling.

3:35 p.m, defense.

He wanted his boys to play harder than their opponents and never be outhustled. He hung a sign above the locker room door that read, "It's not the size of the dog in the fight, but the size of the fight in the dog." Every practice, every game, it reminded them to be tough, to play hard, to want to win more than the other team wanted to win.

He worked hard and put in long hours during the basketball season. When he wasn't teaching and coaching, he scouted other teams. But he didn't let the job absorb him. Yes, he was competitive. He loved to win as much as the next person, but he maintained his own life. He kept things in balance. He enjoyed fishing. He once took his son out on Lake Michigan in a row boat with an on-board motor to catch coho. Three foot waves battered the tiny vessel. "At least one of us got wet, I can tell you that," Mike Adams said.

He enjoyed frying hamburgers and liked to joke with friends that he was the best at the job. He did his best, put in one-hundred percent and things just worked out for him. He believed if you put in hard work, you would be successful.

He loved his players. "Cared about every one of his kids. All you had to do was call him and he'd be there," Mike Adams said.

He was successful at coaching because he sold his players on a lifestyle—not just a game.

Doug Adams took pride in his coaching career, yes, but he took even greater pride in his teaching career. That was what he lived to do. Basketball, football, cross country—it didn't matter. Teaching young men, developing young men, helping them grow—*that* mattered. Being the best teacher he could be—having his boys grow into fine young men who succeeded in life and learned lessons—that motivated Doug Adams.

At one point, Tulane University offered him the position of head basketball coach. It included a significant pay raise and free scholarships for his three children. But Adams knew that most of the players at Tulane would arrive, in their minds, knowing everything and how they wanted to do things. "I'm teaching kids to play basketball and live life," he told his son, Mike. He didn't feel that he'd be doing that at Tulane. He turned down the job.

Good thing for the boys who played for him. Good thing for Michigan City, Indiana.

DAWN OF A NEW SEASON: 1965-66

When the class of '66 moved from junior high to Elston High School at the start of their sophomore year in 1963, Al Whitlow moved with them. He had taken a job at the high school and became Coach Adams' assistant and coached the Pink Imps. In November 1965, the coaching staff had a good feeling about the upcoming season, but no ambition of winning the state.

"We had a pretty good nucleus coming back," Whitlow said, "We knew we had some good ball players. Had good kids. Good attitudes. And had height. We also had speed. We were feeling good about the year, but still it was unbelievable to go through it like we did—in the second half of the year after the holiday tournament."

Height indeed. Of the twelve boys on Elston's varsity roster, only three stood shorter than six feet tall.

Jim Cadwell—6'5, Senior*
Stan Farmer—6'2, Senior*
Fred Leborn—6'1, Senior*
Rob McFarland—6'5, Senior*
Terry Morse—6'5, Senior*
O'Neil Simmon—5'9, Senior*
Calvin George—6'1, Senior
Mike Adams—5'11, Junior
Sam Garrett—6'1, Junior
Larry Gipson—5'9, Junior

Harold Kennedy—6'3, Junior
Dennis Krueger—6'4, Junior
*—returning Letterman

With the roster set, one important point of business had to be meted out before a single home game could be played: the ticket situation. Red Devil Gym sat 4,200 people but basketball games were the hottest ticket in town. Warren Jones set aside 100 tickets for the opposing team. Then, season passes were sold to any student who wanted one. Jones philosophy held strong: it was all about the kids and they got first choice. Period. Remaining tickets went to the public, but demand exceeded supply.

"We were sold out before the season ever started," Jones said. "We had to have drawings for tickets. We never had enough tickets, so before the season started, we had people come and fill out a card and put in the hopper and we drew their names out until the tickets lasted."

November 12, 1965, the doors of Red Devil Gym opened at 6:00 p.m. The parking lot at Elston High School and surrounding street curbs filled with cars. Men and women paced through the brisk dark air and into the crowded auditorium. It was like any game night, but no players ran out onto the court. Upon entering the building, each family filled out a small card with their name and then took a seat in the stands. Each card was collected and deposited into a large cylindrical drum. The drum was taken to the center circle of the court where everybody could see it. Warren Jones commanded the microphone and explained the rules. At 7:00 p.m., someone turned the hand crank, the drum tumbled over and over, cheerleaders took turns drawing cards, and Jones called out the name.

One year, a cheerleader reached in her hand, pulled out a card, and Jones read the name: it was the girl's father. "The crowd whooped and hollered," Jones said. "The poor little cheerleader was so embarrassed."

The drum tumbled, cheerleaders drew names, Jones called out the names. On and on it went until everybody's name was called or there were no more seats left. In years past, the remaining tickets were sold at Arndt's Sporting Goods Store. This year, however, they ran out of tickets before everybody's name was called. While some went home happy and planned out their Friday and Saturday nights, others left disappointed and angry. But nobody could blame the school or Warren Jones of cheating, playing favorites, or impropriety. It had been done in the open for everybody to see.

But Jones noticed a troubling trend. "You should be aware, as we are, that many people are registering more than once and, hence, more than one registration card is appearing in the hopper for a particular person, or family," he told to the press. The next year, a change would be made to disqualify anybody with multiple submissions.

Bill Redfield concurred, "As is usually the case, the fan who tries every angle to get tickets and fails to get the job done is likely to be the one to holler the loudest."

It had been eight-and-a-half months since fans packed Red Devil Gym to cheer on their team. With the ticket situation settled, it was finally time to play basketball.

A SHAKY START

The headline could have read, "The Battle of the Devils." The Red Devils of Michigan City opened the season at home against the number five team in the state: the Gary Froebel Blue Devils. Rob McFarland was limited to a minute or two of play, just to see how his ankle felt. He twisted it something fierce in the very first practice.

"There's a story," McFarland said. "I went to a family doctor and there were just torn tendons and ligaments, and he put the thing in a cast. I was in a cast for about seven days and Doug [Adams] says, 'So what are you doing with that thing?'"

"Well the doctor put it in the cast."

"Dr. Kubik here says that it shouldn't be in a cast."

"Oh."

"'You wanna play,' and I was told to go home and talk to my doctor. I went home, sat in the bathtub and pulled that thing off and just got rid of it and came back. He said, 'I think you'll be OK,' and I started to walk on it a little bit."

With McFarland unable to play, the Red Devils lost another starter halfway through the first quarter. Jim Cadwell suffered a knee injury and had to be helped off the court. The team expected him to miss half the season.

With the exception of the first minute of the game, Gary Froebel led the whole way and beat Michigan City by eight points. Fortunately, the team was rich with talented forwards who could fill in.

Bill Redfield acknowledged the unfortunate injuries to McFarland and Cadwell, but wrote that Coach Doug Adams, "has some coachable boys among the available talent and the Red Devils won't be a pushover for any club."

A week later, Chicago Marshall High School visited Michigan City. The Marshall Commandos won the Chicago Public League championship in 1965 and finished third in the Illinois state tournament. The team returned four of its starting five players, including a top national recruit, Richard Bradshaw, who averaged twenty-one points per game and scored thirty-four against Elston the previous year. But Coach Adams had a plan for Bradshaw.

The boys believed Coach Adams had a sense of humor, but all of them found it hard to get him to crack a smile. All but one, that is. Just ask any one of the former players who was the funniest member of the team and you'll get one answer: Stanley Farmer.

Farmer liked to say, "Yeahhh, Jack!" when agreeing with something he'd heard, or just to acknowledge a conversation of any sort, really. One day in the training room, Coach Adams was talking to Farmer while taping his ankles.

"Yeahhh, Jack!" Farmer said.

"Stanley, you say that again and there's going to be trouble," Adams said.

"Okayyy, Jack!" Farmer replied.

During one practice, Adams blew the whistle and Farmer was on the far end of the gym. Adams held up two fingers and called out, "Stanley, how many fingers am I holding up?"

"Five." Farmer said.

Adams shook his head and asked, "Stanley, if you can't see, how do you know if you have the ball?"

"When I have something cold and wet in my hands," Farmer replied.

Coach Adams just looked at him while the other boys turned away and tried not to laugh. Crazy kid that he was, Adams loved him, and he knew one thing—if he told Farmer, "Don't let that player out of your sight," he would *have* to guard him close.

Against Chicago Marshall, Adams gave Farmer his assignment: "Don't let Bradshaw out of your sight. Wherever he goes—you go."

When Marshall called a timeout, Farmer followed Bradshaw into his team's huddle.

"Hey, what are you doing here?"

"I'm not supposed to let that guy out of my sight," Farmer said.

Marshall's assistant coach escorted Farmer back to the Red Devils bench. "Hey, here's your guy," he said.

Whereas Bradshaw had scored thirty-four against the Red Devils the previous year, Stanley Farmer held him to thirteen. And Richard Bradshaw had to work *hard* for every one of those points. Meanwhile, Terry Morse carried the Red Devils scoring load in the first half and Dennis Krueger scored most of his in the second. They scored twenty-four points apiece and Morse added twenty rebounds. Without Cadwell and McFarland in the lineup, Michigan City beat the highly touted Commandos of Chicago, 93 – 69.

Friday night, the boys traveled to St. Joseph, Michigan, and won handily, 84 – 52.

Bill Redfield wrote, "The Red Devils of Michigan City picked up a lot of boosters over the weekend and they could lose them just as fast this weekend."

Redfield was right. People began to take notice of the Elston Red Devils, but the team still had a rough road ahead. The boys would play the next six games on the road and in the upcoming weekend series, they would play two top-ten teams back-to-back.

On Friday, December 10, Michigan City Elston traveled to South Bend to play the number one ranked team, and fellow Northern Indiana Conference member, South Bend Central Bears. Cadwell was still out and poor Rob McFarland with that lingering ankle injury, missed the game due to the flu. In the first half, Elston fell behind by fifteen points and connected on only twenty-eight percent of their shots. At halftime, The Bears maintained a nine point lead.

When the fourth quarter opened, Elston had cut the lead to three points, but the Red Devils began to lose one player after another—this time to fouls. Farmer fouled out in the third quarter, Krueger fouled out with five minutes to play, and Sam Garrett got his fifth foul with 1:15 left in the game. Eight boys made field goals that night in the team's balanced attack, but the real hero was Calvin George. George—a senior who hadn't made the varsity or JV team the previous year—came off the bench ready to play.

"He had a great night that night and really pulled us through," said Al Whitlow. "He hit some shots from the corner—I can see him to this day—he came in, he had a great shot, and he had a great night that night."

George would score thirty-three points all season, but perhaps the four most important points he scored came late in the fourth quarter against South Bend Central. With fewer than three minutes to play in the game, George's field goal gave Elston the lead, 65 – 63. One minute later, his second basket made it 68 – 65, a lead the Red Devils never lost.

When the final buzzer sounded in South Bend that night—without two key players and three more who fouled out of the game—the Red Devils had upset the top-ranked team in the state of Indiana, 73 – 69. Doug Adams compared the victory to one in 1958 when the Red Devils defeated state champion, Fort Wayne South.

Saturday night, the team travelled to Valparaiso to play the sixth-ranked Vikings. When the game ended, Michigan City snapped Valparaiso's streak of eighteen straight home wins and this time Stan Farmer led the Red Devils with twenty-one points. It was a sweet, and unexpected, present for Coach Doug Adams.

The following day, Adams celebrated his forty-second birthday and two days later, the Associated Press (AP) rewarded Michigan City with the number five state ranking.

For the next two weeks, the team struggled to find consistency. It lost a game at South Bend Adams by eleven points and Bill Redfield wrote, "Michigan City didn't come close to matching last week's sparkling performances."

The next night, McFarland re-entered the lineup and scored twelve points as the team beat Hammond High School.

The last weekend of 1965, the boys played in Elkhart's holiday tournament. They had dropped to tenth in the AP's state ranking and flew past Warsaw, 94 – 71, as Jim Cadwell scored twenty-two points in his first game back from his knee injury. Simmons added twenty; Gipson, fourteen; Morse, thirteen; and Krueger, twelve—more evidence of that balanced attack. The next night, the team led Elkhart, 39 – 30, at halftime, but then went on to lose the game by one point.

The AP dropped them from the top ten rankings.

With six wins and three losses, the team was not where they wanted to be. Sure, it was a winning record and a decent start. Sure, they had suffered injuries and illness to key players, but they had beaten top-ranked teams despite those losses. They also managed to lose to less talented teams.

To win as many games as possible, win the Sectional, and have any chance of getting beyond the Regional, Coach Adams knew that his team needed something. Something to generate a long run like Adams' team had done in his first year as head coach. The answer wasn't clear yet, but Al Whitlow kept talking, talking and Adams kept listening.

A NEW DEFENSE & RED DEVILS ROLL

After the world rang in the new year of 1966, Elston played its first home game in more than a month and defeated the Goshen Red Devils on a Friday night. The following day, the boys boarded a bus and rode 150 miles down Highway 421 to the state capital to play ninth-ranked—and still undefeated—Indianapolis Wood Woodchucks. The Chucks were led by 6'9" center, Greg Northington, and expected to handle the northerly Red Devils on their home court.

If Indianapolis Wood had scouted the Elston Red Devils, there was one thing they never could have anticipated. Adams tried something new and Redfield pointed it out when he wrote, "Northington and his tall teammates forced the Red Devils to use a zone defense for the first time in years and they did a pretty good job."

Adams set aside that strict man-to-man defense and deployed a zone. The team trailed most of the second and third quarters and the game's leading scorer, Jim Cadwell, fouled out with three minutes to play. But McFarland and Krueger combined for thirteen of Elston's nineteen points in the fourth quarter of play. Farmer chipped in fourteen points for the game and 5'9" guard O'Neil Simmons pulled down seven rebounds against the taller Woodchucks.

It was another team effort. Another balanced attack. Elston defeated Indianapolis Wood, 57 – 52.

Adams was pleased with the way his team handled the tough road game and the change in defense. As the boys boarded the bus for home, Adams told them, "You did a great job."

The boys started to click. Every one of them understood his role. Each player was happy to contribute to the team's goal of winning, whether they were called on to play two minutes or thirty-two minutes. They knew each teammate's strengths and limitations. If Simmons got the ball, something good was going to happen. If Cadwell was open, you passed him the ball and waited for him to make the shot. Everybody knew each other. Trusted each other.

"In the end, as long as the score was way ahead of the other guys, *that* was the point," said Cadwell. "We didn't really much care who scored, we just wanted to win."

Back-to-back home games! The city couldn't wait to cheer for its team and finally had the boys all to themselves on Friday and Saturday night. At the high school, a Friday home game meant a pep rally in the afternoon. The entire student body assembled in Red Devil Gym. There were speeches, skits, and cheers. Number one cheerleader, Principal Warren Jones, emceed the event and gave his favorite cheer that wasn't just for the team, but for *all* Elston High School students.

"Is there anybody here from City?" Jones shouted.
Yeah!
"Are we weak?"
No!
"Are we strong?"
Yeah!

"Let's hear that Red Devil roar!"

Exuberant teenagers released 2,300 screams into the auditorium air.

Students knew Mr. Jones and trusted him, but they also knew he maintained discipline and demanded respect and good behavior. As a rule, nothing was to be thrown on the basketball floor. Ever. During a pep rally one year, some kids had crafted paper airplanes and tossed them around in the student section. One airplane caught some air and drifted out of the student section and onto the center of the court. Jones stared at the students, stepped forward, and took the microphone.

"Do you know what these paper airplanes remind me of?" Jones asked.

The assembly grew quiet. Uh-oh, students thought, here it comes.

"It's like the Elkhart Blue Blazers. They are flying very high but as soon as they meet Michigan City, they fall to the ground."

Ho-ho! You go, Principal Jones!

The students laughed and yelled. Yes, he demanded discipline. Yes, he wanted every one of them to get a good education. But remember—he also wanted the kids to have fun. When asked about that story, Jones grinned. "I don't remember that, but that was no place to get upset. You take it and do the best that you can with it."

Friday night. The Elkhart Blue Blazers visited Red Devil Gym and Elston was eager to redeem its holiday tourney loss just two weeks earlier. At 6:30 p.m. the Pink Imps and Blue Blazers JV teams tipped off their game. The varsity players sat behind the bench, dressed in sport coats and narrow, black neckties, patiently waiting for their turn to play. They teased each other and engaged in good-natured ribbing.

Hey, Jim, see you got your crew cut trimmed. Perfectly lined up with the back of your shooting hand. Does that mean you're going to make a few more shots tonight? I sure hope so!

Bill Redfield and other media people had squeezed into the crow's nest nestled between the ceiling and the rafters. Elkhart parents and fans filled the one-hundred seats Jones had set aside for them. By the fourth quarter, the varsity team had left for the locker room and 4,100 Red Devils fans—students and adult season ticket holders—had arrived. They said their hellos and settled into their seats.

To accommodate all of the fans, the school had squeezed every possible seat into the cramped auditorium. They installed bleachers on the main floor. They installed a massive bleacher on the stage behind the far basket that stretched so high that the people in the top row couldn't see the far end of the court because the top of the curtain partially blocked their view. In front of the stage, three or four more rows of bleachers were squeezed in. Bodies pressed tight against the playing floor. As a player inbounded the ball, fans in the first row had to slide their knees to the left and the right to make room for him.

The JV team had fallen behind, so Coach Whitlow put on the 2-2-1 full-court press. The Pink Imps' defense choked the opposing team's offense in the backcourt and they scored some quick, easy points. The crowd grew excited. Riled up. Man, they loved to see that 2-2-1 press in action. Fans stood and yelled with approval. The massive student section pounded their hands and hollered their support.

Come on Red Devils, bury 'em! Bury 'em now!

The energy in the building began to thrum. The noise level increased. When the game ended and Whitlow's Pink Imps exited the floor, anticipation grew to a fevered pitch.

Before the game, student artists spent hours painting a caricature of a Red Devil sticking a pitchfork into the backside of the Blue Blazer mascot, a tense, red-faced madman riding a lightning bolt. They spent another fifteen minutes prior to the game stretching the artwork across an iron ring seven feet in diameter. Two boys now carried the ring onto the court and made a turn, so everyone in attendance could see the art work. Fans nodded and applauded their approval.

The band played, "Rock Around the Clock," as the cheerleaders danced onto the floor and cheered to the beat:

Hey everybody,
It's just about a quarter 'til 8,
Hurry up and don't be late,
Our starting five is really great,
Here they come now. . .

One-by-one, each cheerleader called out the name of a starting player and skipped out onto the floor in formation, keeping rhythm with the music.

Jim Cadwell!
Rob McFarland!
O'Neil Simmons!
Terry Morse!
Fred LaBorn!

After the sixth girl called out, "Coach Adams!" the cheerleaders had formed a V and yelled, "Victory!"

Then, O'Neil Simmons broke through the paper ring and ran out onto the floor to a capacity crowd—all on their feet—that roared its support.

"Once we broke through the hoop, man, they just went wild," Simmons said.

"It was amazing, it really was. It was fantastic. It was one of the greatest feelings a guy could have is to run out—come out there and—the place goes crazy," Cadwell said with a look of awe.

The boys' adrenaline pulsed. They knew that these people had come to see them play that night and they didn't want to let them down. They *were* Red Devils.

Michigan City had just beaten a ranked, undefeated opponent in Indianapolis. They were playing at home in front of a sold-out audience. Everybody was cheering for them. But rather than redeem themselves, the team reverted to its bad form. Rather than moving forward, the Red Devils were stuck in place. Moving backward, even. Passes missed their intended teammates. Shots didn't fall. Things looked bad. How could this be? What was going on?

When he was really upset, when a player made a foolish mistake, or did something Coach Adams didn't like, he'd tear off his glasses and stare at him. That look—you *knew* you were in trouble. Adams abused his thick, dark-rimmed glasses in the first two quarters of the game. Things were not going well. Sitting beside him, Al Whitlow kept talking, talking, talking into Adams' ear, telling him what he saw and feeding him ideas. Adams watched the action on the court and listened to his assistant coach. Whitlow's thoughts jelled with Coach Adams and he made a change here, another change there. On it went.

Elkhart led, 10 – 9, after the first quarter and, 21 – 20, at the half. Going into the locker room for intermission, the thought of getting beat by Elkhart a second time flooded Doug Adams' mind. Meanwhile, the smartest players quickly ran down into the locker room so they could grab a seat in the second row. The further they could sit away from Coach Adams and that chalkboard, the better.

Adams pounded the chalk into the blackboard so hard that broken pieces ricocheted this way and that, splattering the players seated in the front row. If someone's attention drifted off, an eraser, or a piece of chalk hit him and brought him back into the conversation. If Adams were really angry, he'd just throw his glasses at you. You could tell if it had been a rough year by the amount of glue and tape holding his glasses together at the end of the season.

"In the right circumstances, he would yell," said Mike Adams. "He'd raise his voice to make a point and depending on how big the point he needed to get across, that's how loud he would yell."

"He was a very effective communicator," McFarland smiled. "He would get in your grill—it didn't make any difference who it was."

But demean or belittle a player?

"Never."

He expressed his disappointment or frustration. He would dress down the team by talking about their poor play, or address a mistake made. But he never swore, he never insulted a player, and he never called anybody names—these things were not part of his values and he would not do it to his boys. Ever.

Adams was frustrated with the first half of play. He and Whitlow talked it over. The decision made: we're switching defense.

Adams put in the same five players who started against Elkhart in the holiday tournament, but the team experienced a much different result this time around. Bill Redfield wrote,

"The five had a rough go of it until the third quarter when they switched to a zone defense and it forced the Blazers into 16 errors and they got but 8 shots, making only a pair."

That's right—the Red Devils forced Elkhart to make sixteen turnovers and allowed them to make only four points in the third quarter. The Red Devils rolled and the fans went wild, cheering and screaming. During a timeout, Adams had to wait for the crowd to calm down because the boys couldn't hear his voice over their screams no matter how loud he talked.

The cheerleaders led the students in chants,

City's got the pep,
City's got the steam,
City has got,
The best team!
Goooo City!

Throughout the city, thousands of Red Devils fans listened to the broadcast on the radio. Second shifters working in Michigan City's factories tuned in. Old men who didn't have a season ticket and young boys who aspired to be Red Devil basketball players tuned in. Women and girls tuned in. Fans of every color, age, and religion tuned in. This was Michigan City, Indiana, and basketball was their game.

Within minutes, the game was in Michigan City Elston's hands. No longer was Elkhart a threat. No longer was Adams worried about losing two games to the Blue Blazers in the same season. After years of strictly man-to-man defense, Adams deployed a zone and the adjustment was exactly what the team needed.

Al Whitlow, explained the change:

> When you have 6'5", 6'6", and 6'4", and 5'9", and
> 5'9", and you have the bench, you start utilizing

the talent that you have so that you can get the most benefit from it. You make the adjustments.

If I'm a clumsy 6'2" forward—which I was—then I can't chase a 6'4" guy who's got a good shot and I can't get to him in time in a man-to-man, then we need to think about a way to get me out there. So, why don't we start you out here, Al, and you play this wing of the zone. Now you don't have so far to go to get to that guy. And by the way, you're going to get some help from over here and that kind of thing.

That's typically what you have to do, you have to adjust to your talent. I know the 2-3 [zone] was a staple of our defense after that as well as the press. We were able to press too. Change a little personnel and we could press.

When the final buzzer sounded, the pep band erupted into its standard victory song, "Wipeout," and fans filed toward the exits to the powerful beat of the drums.

Final score: 55 – 37, Elston.

The local taverns were quiet during the game as their few patrons quietly drank their beer while they listened to the radio broadcast. Others listened at home or attended the game. Afterward, taverns filled with fans who came out to talk about the action and hash out all the details.

The following night, the crow's nest filled with statisticians and reporters and 4,200 fans again squeezed into Red Devil Gym. The cheerleaders cheered, O'Neil Simmons tore through the paper ring, and the boys ran out onto the floor to a cacophony of screams. The crowd grew so excited the players could barely hear. On the court, 5'9" Larry Gipson replaced Fred LaBorn as a starting guard and he and Simmons combined for thirty-seven points. Twice, when Hammond Noll got the score close, Michigan City turned its 2-2-1 zone press into fast and easy points.

20 – 18.

30 – 18.

38 – 20.

Michigan City won, 96 – 67. The switch to zone defense paid off. The players were all healthy and really starting to jell as a unit. Adams frequently played eight, ten, twelve guys each game. And the twelve young men were the most selfless group of players a coach ever could have asked for.

"We didn't really much care who scored, we just wanted to win."

The team was firing on all cylinders. Weekend after weekend, the Red Devils rolled over opposing teams.

Friday night. They brushed off conference opponent Mishawaka, 77 – 45.

Friday night. They cruised past their arch rival, the LaPorte Slicers, 83 – 67.

Saturday night. Elston pounded the Muncie Central Bearcats, 96 – 53. All twelve players scored.

"It was a great team effort. We had great depth. Teams might stay with us for a half, but by the third quarter, we were blowing them out of the ballgame," Adams said years later.

The team closed out January with a perfect 7-0 record and returned to the top ten rankings. The offense poured in points as it averaged seventy-eight per game. The 2-2-1 press and the zone defense stifled opponents who averaged only fifty-one points per game that month.

In February, the boys continued to roll.

Saturday night. Peru, Indiana. Michigan City, 93 – Peru, 48. Eleven Red Devil players scored.

Friday night. Michigan City, 80 – South Bend Washington, 57. Cadwell, Krueger, and Simmons all had the flu. McFarland led the team with nineteen points.

Friday night. Michigan City Elston, 77 – South Bend Riley, 59. The team locked in the Northern Indiana Conference championship and won its tenth game in a row.

The following afternoon, the boys boarded a bus and traveled to the Berry Bowl in Logansport to finish the regular season schedule.

THE BERRY BOWL

Saturday night at the legendary Berry Bowl in Logansport, the Berries were riding a nine-game home win streak and the hometown fans didn't think much of the Red Devils ten straight wins. Michigan City was, after all, one of those northern teams and not a member of the powerful North Central Conference, they thought.

"The Berries' fans were unimpressed with the Red Devils' record and said in so many words that the North Central Conference has too much class for the upstate teams," Redfield wrote. "It was pointed out, however, that Elkhart, an also-ran team in the Northern Indiana Conference, beat Marion's North Central champions."

The game was intense from start to finish and grew really heated at one point. Adams spotted six Logansport players on the court. At the same time, a referee whistled one of his boys for a personal foul. The officials didn't spot the sixth man and rejected Adams' pleas, but they didn't ignore his protest. Adams undoubtedly stomped his foot and shouted his favorite exclamation when he was angry, "Holy Toledo!" An offended referee blew his whistle and slapped Adams with a technical foul. Logansport made all three subsequent free throws.

Coach Adams was angry, no doubt about it, but he sat down and stifled his frustration. A tight game like this was no time to make matters worse. His team needed him. Besides, he and Warren Jones had an agreement.

"Holy Toledo! He said that once in a while to the referees and got a tech," Jones said, "but Doug and I had an understanding—only one tech, because it riles the crowd. So I would say, 'Okay, Doug, no more than one each game.' He abided by that. He never got more than one tech."

Redfield noted that, "The Berry boosters weren't around after the game but they did make some kind of comments about the Red Devils as they appeared to have the game won. At the same time they got in some digs about Michigan City's big men getting away with fouls."

The fans that Redfield mentioned ignored the fact that Logansport went 11 ½ minutes—including the entire third quarter—without being whistled for a foul and that big men Terry Morse and Rob McFarland fouled out with 5:30 to play. It was a two point game then, but seconds later when Logansport finally did commit a foul, Jim Cadwell's free throw started a two minute burst that gave Michigan City a ten point lead.

When the Red Devils exited the gym along the bleachers, fans tossed popcorn, empty cups, and wadded up programs at them. The strong fourth quarter play and contributions from the bench—at least nine players played and eight of them scored—earned Michigan City Elston its eleventh victory in a row, 77 – 63.

If Redfield was right and Logansport fans considered them not classy, well, Michigan City never claimed to be so. The city by the lake had a nice beach, but it was better-known for making rail cars and steel. It embraced its hard-working, blue-collar character and had no intention of letting that go. The North Central Conference could have its classy image.

The players, fan buses, and fans returned to the city where wicked winds blew off Lake Michigan and lake effect snow blotted out the sun.

The team took pride in breaking Logansport's nine-game home win streak and in its own eleven straight victories. They had a 17-3 record. The AP ranked the Red Devils fifth in the final statewide ranking. It was the last week of February and the state basketball tournament was about to start.

1965-66 Elston Red Devils. Kneeling (L-R): Sam Garrett, Mike Adams, O'Neil Simmons, Bob Hampton (mgr.), Larry Gipson, Fred LaBorn. Standing (L-R): Coach Doug Adams, Harold Kennedy, Dennis Krueger, Jim Cadwell, Terry Morse, Rob McFarland, Stanley Farmer, Calvin George, Asst. Coach Al Whitlow.
Photo by Bob Wilke

Returning starters Simmons, Morse, Cadwell, and Coach Adams.

Terry Morse (50) grabs a rebound against Gary Froebel. Stanley Farmer (left) and Larry Gipson (32) look on.

Dennis Krueger (42) against Gary Froebel.

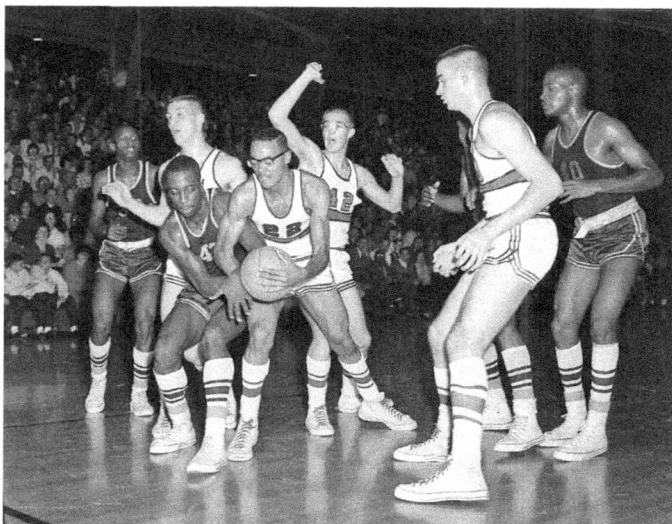

Stanley Farmer (22) battles Richard Bradshaw of Chicago Marshall for the basketball. Photo by Bob Wilke

Fred LaBorn.
Photo by Bob Wilke

Principal Warren Jones leads a pep rally at Elston High School.

Michigan City Mayor, Randall C. Miller, rooting for the Red Devils. (Before the Semi-state, he dyed his beard red.)

Five-thousand fans pack Red Devil Gym at 1:30 a.m. to celebrate the team's
Semi-state championship.

Red Devil cheerleader, Barbara Smith, minutes before
the championship game at the Fort Wayne Semi-state.

Coleen Baker, Vicki Eis, Becky Fritz, Barbara Smith (devil), John Jones, Sharon Szymkowski, Nancy Bobinski, Debbie Winski. Photo by Bob Wilke

Fans on Franklin Street.

A church supports the Red Devils during their State tournament run.
Photo by Bob Wilke

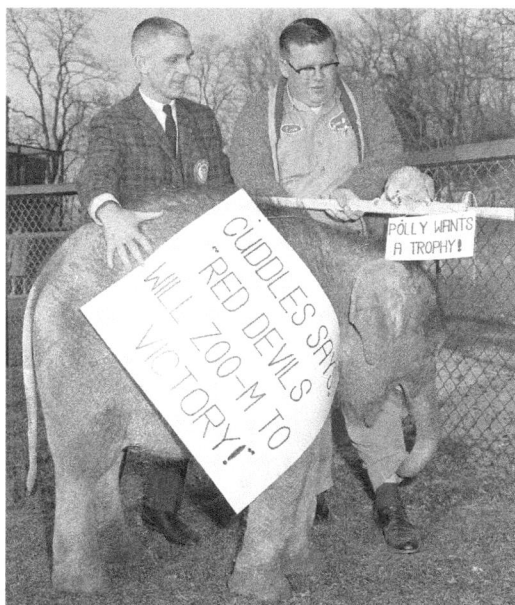

The Michigan City Zoo shows its support for the Red Devils.
Photo by Bill Swedenberg

Red Devil Fans cheer at the State Finals in Indianapolis.

Elston vs. East Chicago Washington. O'Neil Simmons (10), Terry Morse (50), Jim Cadwell (12), and Dennis Krueger (right).

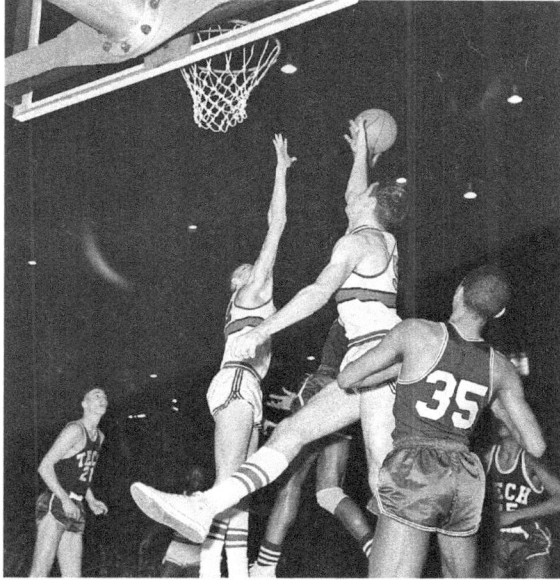

Dennis Krueger (left) and Terry Morse (right) battle for the ball against Indianapolis Tech in the State final.

Asst. Coach Al Whitlow and his wife, Pat, at the State Finals in Indianapolis.

Jim Cadwell (12) in the State championship game (above). Photo by Bill Swedenberg
O'Neil Simmons and Larry Gipson (32) after winning State (below).

Jim Cadwell, the Trester Mental Attitude Award winner, and his family celebrate.

1966 STATE CHAMPIONS

Terry Morse and
O'Neil Simmons.

Elston Red Devils. 1966 State Champions.

The team arrives back in Michigan City. Warren Jones (left), Al Whitlow and Doug Adams (center), cheerleaders and team (right). Photo by Bob Wilke

The team makes its way through the crowd to the victory rally at Ames Field.
Photo by Bob Wilke

The victory rally at Ames Field. Photo by Bill Swedenberg

Coach Adams addresses the crowd while the team is seated to his right.
Photo by Bill Swedenberg

Cheerleaders unveil a
banner.
The team and the State
Championship trophy
are in the background.
Photo by Bill Swedenberg

LITTLE MATTER OF WINNING

February 16, 1966, the pairings for the first level of the Indiana state basketball tournament—the Sectional—were announced on the radio and published in the newspaper. Whereas twelve entrants participated in 1964 and ten in 1965, now eight teams competed in the local Sectional, a number the IHSAA considered ideal. Two games would be played Thursday night, two games Friday night, two games Saturday afternoon, and the championship game would be held Saturday night.

The precarious ticket situation persisted. Michigan City hosted the LaPorte County Sectional tournament and had to share its gymnasium—and its seats—with seven other schools. After high school students got first shot at tickets, only 300 seats remained for Michigan City's general public. Warren Jones scheduled a drawing. The parking lot and street curbs outside the high school filled with cars. Season ticket holders filed into Red Devil gym and wrote their names on cards. The hopper was placed in front of everybody, it tumbled around, cheerleaders pulled out names, and Jones read the names out loud. Many fans went home disappointed and would have to listen to the tournament games on the radio.

While most Red Devils fans considered a Sectional championship a given, Coach Doug Adams took a more measured approach. When asked if this would be the year to finally win a Regional, he replied, "There's a little matter of winning the Sectional before talking about the Regional." As the Pink Imps coach, he witnessed the tiny schools of Union Mills and Rolling Prairie beat Elston to win Sectionals in 1950 and 1951. There was also the question of fellow Northern Indiana Conference member and arch rival, LaPorte— Elston's main threat every year. Adams took the season one game at a time and never overlooked an opponent. Never.

Al Whitlow explained.

> We always were worried [about getting out of the Sectional]. When I was a junior high coach, it was my job to scout LaPorte. If they played, I scouted them. Every weekend. I even remember going down to Knox to scout them.
>
> They were considered to be our number one threat and that's the number one rivalry. So, we wanted to make sure we knew as much about them as we possibly could, so that was one of my jobs: to scout LaPorte.
>
> LaPorte never gave me any season tickets, but I was there quite a bit. If we weren't playing, Doug and I would go scout them. There was scouting [of other teams] going on but, not to that extent.

Elston had beaten LaPorte twenty out of their last twenty-one meetings and if anybody ever wondered how, or why, the extensive scouting was one big reason. As a result, the boys entered the tournament well-prepared and they knew not to take it for granted.

"You know, back in those days, if you were a player for Michigan City and you lost the Sectional, you might as well transfer because you were in a lot of trouble. We knew we had to play hard, but we expected to win the Sectional," Rob

McFarland said. "We got to get to Regionals because we are going to be the first team to get through the damn Regional, *finally*."

As the Sectional opened, Bill Redfield reminded fans no confetti, noise makers, or live mascots were permitted—IHSAA rules. The local newspaper opened the tournament with great fanfare. Basketball themed ads and well wishes filled page after page.

A photo of Jim Cadwell appeared in a Chevy dealership advertisement that read, "SIZZLER! That's JIM CADWELL and the Red-Hot Hand of DEVILS from Elston High."

Herbert Mens Shop "Welcomes ALL Sectional Teams, Fans and Neighbors to Michigan City!" A picture of O'Neil Simmons shooting a basketball sat next to an ad for slim Continentals pants for only five dollars.

Jim's Supermarket featured a photo of Larry Gipson.

The Spaulding Hotel welcomed "All Sectional Tourney Teams! Fans! & Neighbors to Michigan City." In the upper corner, Stan Farmer dribbled a basketball. In the lower corner, it noted that the Flosia Lee Trio would be featured in the Domino Lounge and that all cocktails were fifty cents.

Fred Laborn appeared on an ad that read, "Wallpaper clearance: 25 cents to 98 cents."

In the center of the newspaper was a double page pull-out that included a photo of every team in the Sectional and all of the players' names. A caption read, "May the best team win and go all the way to the 1966 Indiana State Title!"

Players, fans, parents, and visitors loved it.

The Sectional saw no surprises in 1966. All of the favorited teams won games. Thursday night, the Red Devils played its in-city rival, St. Mary's High School, and won by forty-seven points. LaPorte defeated its small school opponent, Westville, by thirty-eight. Friday night, South Central and New Carlisle won their games.

In the Saturday afternoon semi-finals, Michigan City played LaPorte and it was a contrast in philosophies and manpower. The two highest scoring players in the tournament played for LaPorte. They averaged twenty and nineteen points per game and had scored 772 points on the season. Meanwhile, the top two scorers for Michigan City combined for 534 points and no player on the roster ranked higher than ninth in scoring average. But four boys did average double digit points. "There are two ways of looking at it and we hope our way is the best one," Adams said of his team's balanced scoring.

On the locker room chalkboard, Adams had posted the LaPorte player's names, numbers, height, and the scouting report on each one. Who was left-handed. Who didn't like to dribble to his left, who could shoot with either hand, who didn't follow his missed shot, etc., etc. He also matched his players' names with the opponent he would guard. Adams used the scouting reports and had his team prepared, as usual.

Although the LaPorte Slicers jumped out to an early, 10 – 3, lead, the Red Devils soon took over and never looked back. Michigan City won by twenty-one points.

To learn just how strong and how talented the Red Devils were as a team, I called Dave Krider, LaPorte's sports editor at the time. "I hated that team," Krider laughed. It wasn't real hatred, but admiration.

"That was my first year at *The Herald-Argus* and they murdered us in the Sectional. We had two good players and they didn't have much support and they just murdered us. Coming from Elkhart, where I grew up, we had a successful program and won a lot of Sectionals. That was a rude awakening."

In the second game, South Central beat New Carlisle in a game that went down to the wire. That set up a David vs. Goliath matchup for the championship game. with Elston playing the giant's role (South Central had 220 students in grades nine through twelve).

Barry Youngreen played for South Central. "I remember the pregame speech Coach [Morrie] Goodnight gave us," he said. "They play on the same length floor, put their trunks on one leg at a time and all that. But after the game—I questioned that. They had a terrific full court press and Goodnight had it figured out. That didn't bother us—we were able to get the ball up the court. But we couldn't put it in the basket once we got down there."

The Red Devils took an early lead that grew steadily over thirty-two minutes of play. The Elston Red Devils breezed to victory, 88 – 49. After the game, the boys shook hands with their opponents. They cut down one of the nets and posed for pictures. The Elston cheerleaders, a valuable part of the team and school's efforts, cut down the other net.

And with that, Michigan City Elston won its fifteenth consecutive Sectional championship.

NEXT YEAR IS HERE

The last time the Elston Red Devils lost a Sectional, members of the senior class were three years old.

The last time Elston won a Regional, sixteen teams advanced to the State Finals instead of just four. The game included a center jump after every made field goal. Dennis Krueger's dad, Louis, played on the team. Terry Morse and Jim Cadwell's fathers were twelve year olds. It had been thirty-one years and the dreaded hex crept into everyone's mind.

"That was on our minds all the time," said Elston junior Dave Milcarek. "The old jinx. We'd win the Sectional and that's all the further we'd go. We're not going to win the Regional. That was always the story. We always thought we were not good enough to get past the Regional."

The Regional route hadn't gotten much easier than it was in the old Calumet meat grinder. In game one, Michigan City would play Elkhart for the third time and on Elkhart's home court. If they got past the Blue Blazers, they expected to face the number two team in the state: the South Bend Central Bears. Most sportswriters favored the Bears to win the Regional and the whole statewide tournament for that matter. No, it wasn't going to be easy.

Basketball practice continued as usual. Coach Adams worked from his notecards that ticked off the minutes and what the boys worked on.

Monday: fundamentals.

Tuesday: offense, defense, rebounding.

Wednesday: scrimmage.

Thursday: game plan.

The zone defense keyed the Red Devils' success through their fourteen game win streak. Adams used what he had learned from the two games against Elkhart, as well as the scouting report his coaches had developed, to prepare his boys.

Since Elkhart had one of the largest gymnasiums in the nation, the ticket situation eased some. From Elston's allotment of 2,300 tickets, students, faculty, and parents of the players took 1,500. That left 800 to season ticket holders.

Wednesday night, fans filed into the Red Devil Gym at 6:30 p.m. People filled out cards. An hour later, the crank on the hopper turned, cards tumbled inside, cheerleaders drew names, and Warren Jones called out the lucky lottery winners.

Friday before the Regional, the school held a pep rally. The gym filled with 2,300 students and Jones wanted to hear from them.

"Is there anybody here from City?"

Yeah!

"Are we weak?"

No!

"Are we strong?"

Yeah!

"Let's hear that Red Devil roar!"

Yaayyyy!

Coach Doug Adams dressed as King Dom in a cape and Viking-styled crown, introduced his royal court of Red Devils and addressed the subjects—err, students—of Devil Kingdom. Mayor Randall C. Miller spoke briefly. Then the school held a short parade through town.

Although Coach Adams never talked about the Regional hex, he actually was worried. Bill Redfield visited his house that evening and Adams told him the boys "had looked too good in practice. I just wonder if we have overlooked anything," he said more than once. Later, he decided that his boys were ready.

Saturday morning, sixteen school buses filled with students left for Elkhart to cheer on the Red Devils. Over 7,000 fans attended the basketball Regional in Elkhart that year. Elston fans dressed in red and white and nobody could miss Mayor Miller. His goatee and waxed moustache always stood out, but he completed his ensemble with a straw skimmer hat with a giant Red Devils button on the front, a sport coat with a giant MC embroidered on it, and his pants cuffs tucked into red socks.

South Bend Central and Warsaw tipped off at 11:30 a.m. Bill Redfield's prediction that Central would have it easier than Michigan City were quickly dispelled. Warsaw led the game after three quarters and Central won on a basket made with two seconds left in the game. But a win is a win and South Bend Central advanced.

Michigan City and Elkhart tipped off at 12:45 p.m. and the Red Devils quickly demonstrated that they were, indeed, prepared. They led, 19 – 8, and then, 35 – 18, at the half. In the third quarter, the lead quickly grew and Adams rested his starting five as the team cruised to an easy victory. Things looked good, but Michigan City fans had been here before.

They still faced a difficult opponent. The South Bend Central Bears had amassed twenty-one wins, the same as Michigan City, and would not give up without a fight.

The championship game tipped off at 7:15 p.m. and aired on channel 22, WSBT television. Fans might have been nervous about the Regional hex, or concerned about playing the second-ranked team in the state, but the players were not rattled. They wanted to win. They wanted to break the hex. And they felt good about their chances.

Terry Morse still remembered the 1965 Regional and the scoreboard that showed South Bend Washington up by ten points. He remembered the seniors burying their tears in towels.

> Our junior year is when we went to Elkhart for the first time and losing there in the afternoon was probably a little fire underneath us for our senior year. It is sad when you lose the Regional and to watch the seniors cry and be emotional about it. You're emotional, but I get to come back next year. It is kind of a relief a little bit.
>
> When you're there your senior year, things change a little bit. Of course, we had a better team than we had previous to that too, but I think that year before was kind of an inspiration.

Number two versus number five. The Regional championship on the line. In one hour, one team would advance to the Semi-state and one would go home in defeat. Outside, a blizzard raged. Inside Elkhart's Memorial Gym, basketball heated up. Everyone focused on the ten boys, dressed in shorts, jerseys, and Chuck Taylor All Star sneakers. Hands pounded. The air was hot. The game was about to begin.

From the opening tipoff, South Bend Central pressed Michigan City Elston, but Elston turned it into several easy layups and jumped out to a 10 – 1 lead. Central came back and led by one point. Right before the half, the game was tied, but two free throws and a field goal lifted the Red Devils at the half, 30 – 26.

The third quarter went back-and-forth, back-and-forth. In the fourth quarter, South Bend tied the game, 55 – 55. Elston responded with six points in sixty seconds. Cadwell and Morse combined for thirty-two of the team's forty-nine—yes, *forty-nine*—second-half points.

When the game concluded, South Bend Central led nearly every statistical category. They took more shots than Michigan City (85-58). They committed fewer turnovers (10-22). They outrebounded Michigan City (44-41)—something only two other teams had done all season.

Ahh, but the defense—that was the difference maker. Michigan City hit fifty percent of its field goals and held South Bend Central to only thirty-four percent.

Final score: Michigan City, 79 – South Bend Central, 72.

Hex, jinx, curse—call it what you want. It was over. Dead. Done. The boys had broken it.

After the game, school superintendent, A.K. Smith, pointed out the snow storm had made the roads bad and suggested the team take it slow going home.

"We won't be on the road—we'll be flying!" Coach Adams replied.

Some of the buses struggled to get up Bendix Hill on the way home as sixteen fan buses and the team bus slipped and slid through the snow back to Michigan City.

On the team bus, Al Whitlow remembered everybody being happy and one of the kids playing, "How Sweet It Is" by Marvin Gaye on a radio. The bus's tires trudged through the accumulating snow and as the team approached Michigan City, fans turned out to greet them. An elderly woman held a hand-lettered sign and flicked a flashlight on and off at the passing bus. A service station fired a miniature cannon— KABOOM! Everybody knew the team was near. Porch lights flicked on and off. People stumbled out into the snow to wave at the bus.

When it arrived at the gym, a sea of people had amassed inside Red Devil Gym. An impromptu celebration kicked off at 11:30 p.m. in front of 3,000 fans. The cheerleaders grabbed Coach Adams and carried him onto the stage. Adams laughed nervously, hoping they wouldn't tear him limb-from-limb or worse yet, drop him on the floor.

Jones emceed the event, praised the cheerleaders and fans, and turned the microphone over to the team. When he handed it to Al Whitlow, only one thing came to his mind: Marvin Gaye. He exclaimed, "How sweet it is!" and brought the house down as fans went crazy yelling and screaming.

"That's all I could say that night. I was speechless. People who know me know that was very rare for me," Whitlow laughed.

Adams asked the fans, "Would you believe?" and told the crowd he thought the team could go all the way to the State championship. As always, Jones led a few cheers, including one he'd just invented, "Hey, hey, all the way! Hey, hey, all the way!"

"It wasn't planned," Jones told me, "it just came out at the pep rally. The kids loved it. When we had our pep session (it was a three-year high school) the sophomores would go with 'Would you believe,' the juniors would say, 'How sweet it is,' and the seniors would say, 'Hey, hey all the way!' We did that at the pep rally. It was a lot of fun."

Monday's headline read, "Next Year Is Here for the Red Devils." Thirty-one years. Nineteen Sectional championships in that span of time including fifteen in a row. Finally. *Finally*, the frustration had come to an end. Michigan City Elston was Regional basketball champions.

Mayor Miller ordered a sign that read, "Devils All The Way!" and strung it across Franklin Street. He suggested townspeople wear red and white all week to celebrate and support the team and that people should decorate their cars in Elston's school colors. Citizens gleefully obliged.

"You couldn't go to a store and buy anything red and white," Dave Milcarek said. "It was all gone. Signs were everywhere. Go Big Red. State All the Way. Signs in every window of a car. Honking horns. Going up and down Franklin."

The high school cancelled classes Monday and townspeople buzzed with excitement. Merchants ran out of anything red or white they had in stock. Paint stores shook cans of paint all day long. Print shops struggled to keep up with demand for banners and signs and anything—paper, bed sheets, cardboard boxes—anything was painted red and white as people flittered about with excitement.

While all of this went on, a serious matter needed to be addressed. For years, Bill Redfield and his assistant, Roger Bixler, had driven Highway 20 to the Calumet Regional tournament. Every year, they passed The Spa, a high end restaurant in Porter, Indiana, tucked next to the Little Calumet River. Redfield would say that if only they'd won the

Regional, they could have stopped there to celebrate. If we do ever win, he told Bixler, I'll buy dinner.

Year in and year out, the two men drove to the Calumet Regional. Year in and year out, Redfield made the claim. Year in and year out, they lost.

Well, it finally happened and Bixler reminded Redfield of his promise. Redfield tried to wiggle out of it, "Well, I meant the Calumet Regional. We won the Elkhart Regional," he protested. But Bixler wouldn't let up and Redfield relented.

Monday night when basketball practice ended, Redfield, Bixler, Doug Adams and their wives loaded into a large, square sedan and drove to The Spa on a cold, foggy night. They enjoyed appetizers, salads, and steaks. Surely, Redfield must have grown a little nervous by the mounting bill, but he lucked out on the bar tab. The restaurant owner knew who they were and what they were celebrating. Every time the party ordered a drink, the owner delivered it with a flourish:

"This round is from the mayor of LaPorte!"

"This round is from the mayor of Elkhart!"

"This round is from the mayor of South Bend!"

The party of six laughed, and cried, and had a great time. After all, it wasn't every year you won a Regional.

COFFEE, ANYONE?

Michigan City received 1,844 tickets for the Fort Wayne Semi-state. Many people expected student ticket requests to drop from the Regional, but there was no such luck. Twelve-hundred students—over half the student body—paid for tickets to attend the Semi-state tournament 120 miles away.

When somebody asked Warren Jones about tickets—and somebody was always asking about tickets—he had a ready response: "Just be there for the drawing." After Jones took care of students, parents, faculty and the school board, only 300 tickets remained for the adult drawing held Thursday night. The cards, the hopper, the cheerleaders drawing names—it was a familiar routine. Many fans went home disappointed that night.

The state basketball tournament continued like clockwork. The teams had one week to prepare for the next level. As far as basketball practice was concerned, nothing changed at Elston High School.

Monday: fundamentals.

Tuesday: offense, defense, rebounding.

Wednesday: scrimmage.

Thursday: game planning.

The classrooms were another story as teachers improvised their lesson plans to accommodate students who were just too, too excited.

"Next week in classes, you really didn't have to do anything," said Rob McFarland. "They wanted us to be rested. A lot of attention. They shut down the school for the pep sessions when we left for Semi-state."

Friday morning, the school held a pep rally at 9:00 a.m. Sophomores, juniors, and seniors chanted the school's new cheer.

Would you believe!
How sweet it is!
Hey, hey, all the way!
Would you believe!
How sweet it is!
Hey, hey, all the way!

Afterward, the team boarded a bus and headed east. When they reached Warsaw, they saw a sign from Highway 30 that read, "Go, Go Michigan City!" The bus pulled in and the team ate at Horn's Restaurant where former Elston Coach Ick Osborne joined them and wished them luck. Then, they were off to Fort Wayne.

The team felt good about its chances of winning.

"We were just a bunch of dumb high school kids just going out and playing," said Rob McFarland. "I think we certainly didn't go there to lose and I think we had a lot of confidence. You know, after getting all of the scout reports and all the rest of the stuff. I don't even remember being afraid of playing a team or thinking we are the underdogs."

"We always came in like we were going to win," added O'Neil Simmons." We always thought *they* were after *us*."

"Exactly. Adams never talked about if we were underdogs," said McFarland. "We did our zone, we ran our offense, we did our thing and they adjusted to us."

The AP's top basketball reporter, Ron Gilbert, wasn't convinced that Michigan City had the upper hand. He picked them to beat Kokomo in the afternoon game, sure, but he chose Anderson to win the championship game Saturday night.

It was a strange weekend for the boys. When they returned from practice at the Memorial Coliseum, somebody threw a bowling ball through a small window to one of the boys' rooms.

"That was kind of weird," said Terry Morse. "The other thing that was weird was when we went to the practice. The Coliseum was an ice rink. We never played there. They had a hockey team and there's ice and it's cold!"

"They had pallets of stuff, and they were only a couple inches thick, well, they're putting a floor up and stuff to walk on—on the ice. You were walking on ice," said Jim Cadwell.

Employees hadn't finished covering the ice rink with the basketball floor yet. The air was cold and uncomfortable as the boys shot around and went through their drills.

"It looked like it was a postage stamp and all the way around, there was nothing but ice," Morse said.

A couple of errant basketballs left the court and bounced out into the rink. When the student managers chased the balls down, they slipped on the ice and fell on their butts.

"I thought, 'I am not looking forward to this tomorrow,'" Morse said.

Anderson High School played Fort Wayne South in the 11:30 a.m. game Saturday morning. Michigan City played the Kokomo High School Wildcats, who appeared in their eighth Semi-state in nine years. The Wildcats were led by 6'7" center, Mark Gabriel, who averaged nineteen points and seventeen rebounds per game.

"The only thing I remember about going to the Semi-state is another bus trip, which we were used to, and then breakfast and for some reason—who decided that it was the right time to start drinking coffee?" McFarland asked.

"Might've been me. Toast and coffee," Jim Cadwell laughed as he shook his head.

"I just remember at the pre-game we had coffee because we were running big guys in and out of there like crazy. What the hell is wrong? And Whitlow was like, 'They had *coffee*, *COFFEE*? Who drinks coffee?'"

"That is when our bench really came together," Morse said.

"I had four fouls in the first half," said Simmons.

Perhaps the biggest game in Elston basketball history up to that date, and the morning of the games the boys decided to introduce coffee to their teenage metabolism for the first time in their lives. Yep, just a bunch of dumb high school kids, alright.

As the boys got dressed in the locker room and prepared to take the floor for their game against Kokomo, they still expected to skate across ice in a cold coliseum to reach the playing floor. When a voice announced the team over the loud speaker, the boys ran out and things looked different. The ice was gone. It had been covered with a floor and seats. And the air was warm, not cold. The boys liked it much better and relaxed.

But the coffee didn't pay any good dividends to the Red Devils. In the first half of the game, they got outrebounded and shot a paltry thirty-one percent from the floor. Guards Simmons and Gipson kept the team in the game as the big men started out shooting a collective 0-16.

"I was *not* having a good game," Cadwell said. "I couldn't hit anything! I don't know what the hell! Probably that damn coffee!"

Kokomo led by five points at halftime. After believing this was the year they could win it all, and saying so publicly at the post-Regional victory rally, Coach Adams' team was not playing up to its potential. In the locker room the boys dodged bits and pieces of chalk that ricocheted off the chalkboard.

"We were struggling a little bit with Kokomo for a while there and here again, that bench came through for us," Al Whitlow said. "I remember Stan Farmer coming off the bench, grabbing some rebounds, getting fouled, throwing down about four free throws in a row. We just had fluidity on that team and everything was working right. Some guy's having a tough night and put somebody else in—that's why you call it team."

Team, indeed. Farmer and Dennis Krueger came off the bench and made the difference in the game. In the second half, Farmer held Kokomo's 6'7" center to three points, while Krueger scored ten points and grabbed thirteen rebounds. Late in the third quarter, Michigan City finally took a one-point lead and eventually won, 90 – 81.

The night game didn't get any easier.

"Quite honestly, I think Anderson was the best team we played that year," Whitlow said. "At least they were that night. Boy, they were good. Those teams were all good."

Anderson High School had a rich basketball history with three State championships and a pair of runner-up finishes. They finished the regular season ranked fourth in the state in 1966.

More than 9,000 people attended the Semi-state game that night in Fort Wayne. While the teams ran through their pre-game warmups for the championship game, Anderson's mascot dressed in a traditional Indian costume, including a marvelous head-dress that extended to the floor, stood with his arms crossed in the center circle of Memorial Coliseum. Elston cheerleader Nancy Bobinski turned to Barbara Smith, the team's Red Devil mascot, and asked her, "Are you going to let them get away with that?"

Dressed in a red and white houndstooth outfit and sporting little devil horns and a tail, "the world's most heavenly devil" made her way out to the center circle. She eyed the majestic Anderson mascot, and made a circle around him. Then, she stepped into the circle, bumped him in the behind with her hip, forcing him to take a step forward and share the spotlight. Red Devil fans roared. No doubt, Kokomo and Fort Wayne South got a kick out of it too.

When the game began, the score was tight from start to finish and everybody pitched in. Sam Garrett came off the bench and helped guide the team to a lead after Simmons committed three fouls in forty-five seconds. Morse hit six of six field goals in the last quarter and grabbed eleven rebounds. Gipson went a perfect ten for ten from the free throw line. The team led at the end of every quarter: 28 – 24, 49 – 44, 69 – 66, 90 – 80.

Elston won its eighteenth straight game and was headed to the State Final Four for the first time in school history.

It was a momentous event and fans everywhere listened in. Elston graduates as far away as Buffalo, New York, and Atlanta, Georgia, picked up the live broadcast on WOWO radio out of Fort Wayne. After the game, they called friends and relatives back home.

In Michigan City, the entire city tuned into the local radio station, or turned on channel 22, which aired both games on the television. As soon as they had won, everybody knew it and the celebrations commenced. By the time the team returned home, Michigan City hadn't stopped celebrating and they were eager to see the boys return. Another late night celebration awaited. A late, late night celebration.

It was 1:30 a.m. and people burned flares, waved sparklers, and honked horns as the team bus rolled into town. Five-thousand people filled Red Devil Gym. Waiting. Most of them had arrived before midnight. It was standing room only. All of the seats were taken, the concourse filled with fans, and more people crowded onto the gym floor. A small group of band members marked the team's arrival and played their instruments as the players squeezed through the packed auditorium to get to the stage. Someone held a giant sign that read, "ET TU BARATTO!" It alluded to East Chicago Washington head coach, Johnnie Baratto, Michigan City's next opponent and bitter rival.

The boys couldn't believe the scene. It was the middle of the night, they thought. Didn't these people have someplace to be?

"They were on the floor, this solid mass of humanity. It was crazy. It was nuts!" Morse said.

Due to the late hour, only three members of the team addressed the audience: student manager Bob Hampton, Al Whitlow, and Doug Adams. Adams said he was happy he did "a better job of guessing" to lead the team to victory. Superintendent A.K. Smith sent word that Monday's classes at the high school were cancelled yet again in honor of the team's victory.

"I will tell you, the whole next week, there was no school, there was a couple of days off, it was ridiculous," added McFarland.

"That is why we were so popular," Morse laughed.

"I'd get that question, 'You think if we win state, we'll get Monday off?' Yeah. I know I will!" McFarland laughed.

HEY, HEY, ALL THE WAY!

Monday morning, high school students crowded the sidewalk outside the high school waiting to enter the lottery to get a ticket to the State finals. Even though Hinkle Fieldhouse on the Butler University campus sat 14,900 people, the IHSAA gave Elston High School a mere 1,000 tickets.

There would be no drawing in Red Devil gym that week.

Jones set up twenty school buses to take the kids to the game, and a couple days in advance, Michigan City Police made a dry run, mapping out the route and coordinating gas stops for the buses. The route was kept secret to avoid potential danger if too many cars followed. The convoy of student buses would be escorted by six officers in two patrol cars.

Practice resumed its normal routine.

Monday: fundamentals.

Tuesday: media day—wait, what? Yes, a change in routine! The team did take time from its usual schedule, as did all four state finals teams, for a press day. Coach Adams never let his boys talk to the press, "I will talk to the press," he told them, but on press day, he relented and the media was allowed to ask simple questions.

A sports reporter from WSBT-TV, channel 22 out of South Bend, had a camera fixed on Terry Morse.

"All year, who was the toughest center you played against?" he asked.

"Harold Kennedy," Morse replied.

"Cut," the reporter instructed his camera man. "Who is Harold Kennedy?"

"That guy right there. Number twenty-four. My teammate."

"No, I mean an actual player you played against."

"I play against him every day. Look at him—do you want to play against him every day?"

The reporter shook his head. "OK, let's go onto the next question."

"He was tough to get around," Morse told me. "Brutal ball."

Wednesday: scrimmage.

Thursday: game planning.

As each week passed, more and more Michigan City residents wanted to get in on all the hoopla. Red and white clothing, signs, decorated cars. There were signs displayed in windows and hanging from awnings and on walls.

The fire station used all of the window squares of its massive garage doors to spell out, "GO, GO, GO! DEVILS ALL THE WAY!"

Junior high students painted banners that read, "2-4-6-8. Devil's going down to State!"

A storefront window had two giant devil heads and a masthead that read, "RED DEVILS A GO-GO!" Below it was a large team photo and underneath it said, "The Incomparable Red Devils."

The local utility company, NIPSCO, had life-sized, color, cardboard cutouts of the players, coaches, student managers, the athletic director, and Principal Jones standing behind the store front, plate glass window of its main office.

Someone painted, "GO CITY," on telephone poles.

The Louis Krueger residence had a "go DEVILS" neon sign hung above a side door.

Children cut out photos of the players in the local newspaper, then pasted them into the windows of their houses.

One kid painted five large sheets of paper and hung them from his parents' front porch:

"Hey-Hey—What Ya' Say—City's Going—All the Way!"

He drew a picture of Indiana on the fifth sheet and put a star in the center for Indianapolis.

"GO-CITY-GO!"

"GOOD LUCK, CITY!"

"Victory All the Way! Nothing Can Stop Us Now!"

"Hey, Hey, All the Way!"

The signs were everywhere. You couldn't move or breathe without seeing a sign. If you stuck to the streets, you'd still see signs. A couple girls painted "All the way in 66!" on their car's fenders and "All The Way!" on the trunk.

One of the fan buses used to take students to the State championships had the players' names painted on its sides and "GOGO CITY GO!" painted on the tires. *The tires!*

When the team traveled to away games, they didn't ride in a standard yellow school bus. Instead, the school chartered a commercial bus. Friday morning, the boys boarded a bus that would take them to Indianapolis for practice. Terry Morse sniffed the air and looked around quizzically. What is that? It smelled like a new car. He and the boys took their seats. The driver boarded and made his announcement.

"Thank you for riding Indiana Motor Bus. I will be taking you to Indianapolis today for the State tournament and stay with you throughout the duration of your trip and bring you back home on Sunday. This is a brand new bus making its maiden voyage. Enjoy the ride, boys."

When the boys reached Hinkle Fieldhouse, a slew of reporters met them. The boys felt like thousands of eyeballs watched them nonstop as they practiced, shot around, and tried to get accustomed to the playing floor. Fortunately, the boys were getting used to the attention, so it didn't faze them much. "And we were starting to like it," Simmons said.

As for Adams, he told a team of reporters, "I wouldn't mind it every year."

It sure beat sitting at home watching somebody else play.

Adams never talked about the Regional hex because he felt they had always been beaten by better teams. Leading up to State, though, he *did* talk about East Chicago. He made it clear to the boys that East Chicago Washington had beaten Elston in the Regional four times in seven years. He wanted the boys to know. And his message rang through loud and clear.

The two ranked teams in the State finals, fifth-ranked Michigan City Elston (24-3) and seventh-ranked East Chicago Washington (23-4), played at 11:30 a.m. The largest high school in the state, Indianapolis Tech(24-3) with nearly 5,000 students, played Cloverdale (27-1) with 225 students at 12:45.

Elston finally became the favorite to win. Ron Gilbert, who repeatedly wrote that Anderson High School would win State, switched his pick to Michigan City. Members of the Indiana Sportswriters and Broadcasters Association held their annual meeting and fifty of the ninety-six attendees chose

Elston to win it all. Thirty-one voted for Indianapolis Tech. Cloverdale and East Chicago Washington got nine and six votes respectively.

Early Saturday morning, twenty school buses left Elston High School and started the slow, steady trip to the state capital. The long stream of yellow buses filled with students drew onlookers.

"You go through the small towns between here and Indianapolis, people would be out in the streets waving at us, cheering us on so to speak, like Francesville and Medaryville," Jones said. "We had twenty buses, so it took us awhile to get through those small towns. Each student bus had thirty-six students on it, two chaperones, and a bus driver. So there were thirty-nine people on each bus."

But nobody got a ticket until they reached Indianapolis.

"I didn't give them a ticket until they got off the bus because I was afraid that they would scalp them to some gray haired fella and I didn't want him in the middle of my cheer block," Jones said. "So, when they got off the bus at Butler Fieldhouse, they got a red and white pom-pom and a ticket. The way those kids barged into that Butler Fieldhouse, you would have thought they owned it. The amazing part of it all was that I got them home safe."

Meanwhile, the boys stayed at the Motor Inn in downtown Indianapolis. For breakfast, they drank milk and orange juice—everybody stayed away from the coffee. When the time arrived, they rode their charter bus to Hinkle Fieldhouse and entered the locker room. There, the boys developed an entirely new motivation to win. Terry Morse told the story:

> You could only dress ten back then and we had twelve on the team. When it comes to the

Sectionals, two guys had to sit the bench. [Doug Adams] picked out Fred LaBorn and Calvin George. He told Fred that if by chance we were to get lucky and get to the State finals, he told him he would dress for that as he was a senior starting guard at one time.

So, we go through the Sectionals, and we go through the Regionals, and we go through the Semi-state, and we get down to State. We get to the first game and the managers are always there ahead of us and they always had our uniforms laid out in front of the lockers for us.

We get in there and I find mine and right next door, here's Fred's. Fred's in the corner, chewing gum, and one of us said, "Fred, come here, here's your uniform," and he looked at it and he said, "I can't." The place kind of got quiet, but Doug said, "Remember, I promised you." Everybody is listening and he says, "I promised you that if we get to state you can dress."

Fred said, "Listen, we got this far with me not dressing, I'm not going to spoil it—you dress the best ten players."

And everybody was just—wow.

Fred LaBorn had lost his starting guard spot midway through the season. He shot well in practice, yes, but tensed up in games. Thereafter, he dutifully played the role of the opposing team's best shooter in practice, but fell to the bottom of the roster when game time came.

"That story tells you a lot about Fred and a lot about the team too," Rob McFarland said.

"Then we wanted to kick East Chicago's ass!" Morse said.

Elston beat their long-time nemesis from the northwest corner of the state, 81 – 64.

In the locker room after the game, LaBorn told the team, "See, I told ya!"

"That was fun," McFarland said. "It was probably the best game we played all year."

The East Chicago Washington team and head coach Johnnie Baratto entered the Red Devils' locker room after the game. Coach Baratto congratulated the Red Devils, gave a small pep talk, and encouraged them to go on and win state. Each of the players wished them luck and told them they'd be rooting for them.

In the Elston cheer block, consensus among the students was clear: we beat East Chicago, now we *have* to win it all.

In the afternoon game, Indianapolis Tech Titans defeated the peoples' choice, Cloverdale, 58 – 51. There was nothing left for the winning players to do, but go back to their hotel, eat, and get some rest for the night's game. But none of them could sleep. They were too excited for that.

The State championship game tipped off at 7:15 p.m. Nearly 15,000 fans crowded into the fieldhouse and stared down onto the court. The sunlight that had shone through the windows from up high and gleamed off the hardwood floor during the day session had given way to darkness. No distractions remained. Nothing left to focus on now, but basketball.

Elston dressed in white uniforms with a thick stripe below the number. White socks pulled up to the knee and three red stripes mid-shin. Indianapolis Tech wore dark green uniforms and dark crew socks with three white stripes that peeked out just above their sneakers.

The first quarter was marked by sloppy play from both teams—stage fright and nerves showed. The ball went back and forth, up and down the court, and the boys chased after it. Great jump shots from both teams, especially Mike Price of Tech and Cadwell of Elston, interspersed the hectic play.

Jim Cadwell—6'5", 170 pounds. Skinny as a rail, but put a ball in his hands and he became smooth. Lithe. Morse's play was solid. Krueger and Farmer had beautiful jump shots.

In the second quarter, Michigan City calmed down. Played cleaner, smoother. Talking about the guards, Simmons and Gipson, Al Whitlow told me, "They were so quick it was scary." He wasn't kidding. Simmons made the Tech guards look like they were moving in slow motion. He stole the ball, was gone in a flash, and scored an easy layup.

Fouled as the buzzer sounded, Cadwell hit two free throws on an empty court to tie the score at halftime, 30 – 30.

The game was sharp in the third quarter. The back-and-forth picked up, the game got quicker. The boys played tighter. Passes, crisp. Rebounds cleared. Few mistakes. There was plenty of time to play when Cadwell sank his sixth field goal and seventh free throw for nineteen points. Tech struggled to make a basket and were outscored, 18 – 8, in the third quarter.

48 – 38, Elston.

Tech started the fourth quarter with a full court press. Elston turned it over.

Tech forced another turnover, but played sloppy on its own offensive end and still couldn't make a basket.

Fast break—Cadwell to Gipson to Simmons. Rebound—two passes—two dribbles. Bang! Bang! Bang! Simmons laid it in with ease. It was a thing of beauty.

56 – 39, Elston.

Then, Tech came back.

56 – 43.

56 – 46.

56 – 47.

56 – 48.

Fifty seconds left to play. Elston survived Tech's flurry of points. Simmons shot six for six from the free throw line in the fourth quarter and left the game with seconds to play. Fans stood and cheered as he took a seat on the bench. The game was firmly in Elston's grip.

Final score: 63 – 52.

Michigan City Elston—1966 Indiana state basketball champs.

After the game, athletic director Elmer Millbranth was so excited, he raced over to the WIMS radio broadcast table and summed up what everyone in Red Devil land was feeling.

"Heyieyayeay!" Millbranth yelled into the microphone. "We did it! We are the state champs. They did a marvelous job. Twenty in a row. That's it right there! Twenty-six victories and three defeats. Tech picked us up all over the floor the last quarter, but we were able to hold them off. Right. I gotta go out there on the floor. I'll see you in Michigan City!"

Fans stayed and celebrated as the team received its championship rings and the championship trophy. Tournament officials shocked Jim Cadwell when an IHSAA representative presented him with the Trester mental attitude award.

Members of the press praised Elston, but nobody captured the team's play better than the *Hammond Times* and *Chicago Sun-Times* newspapers.

"If you were going to build a perfect high school basketball team what is there about Michigan City that you would change?" asked *Hammond Times* sports editor, Loren Tate.

The *Sun-Times* sports page noted, "the Red Devils of Coach Doug Adams also became only the third team in the 56-year history of Indiana's famed hardwood spectacle to win the title with a zone defense. Only Bloomington in 1919 and Jasper in 1949 went all the way with a zone and Red Devils stuck with it throughout to notch their 20th consecutive victory."

The majority of Red Devils fans were back home in Michigan City. Every house, tavern, and business tuned into the live broadcast of the basketball game on the television or radio. As soon as the game ended, people raced outside into the spring air. They turned on all their lights and flicked porch lights on and off. They hollered at neighbors, "We did it!" yelled in the streets, "Yaaa-hooo!" danced with sparklers, lit off firecrackers, and launched bottle rockets into the night sky. People and cars mobbed Franklin Street, the main business district. Everyone wanted to be there, together, to share their joy and excitement.

Vern Hundt, a graduate of South Central High School and a freshman at Purdue, watched the game on TV in the commons area of his dormitory. As soon as it ended, he and three friends jumped in a car and raced up Highway 421 to Michigan City just to be a part of it all. Ninety minutes after the game ended, they still found quite a scene.

"People were waiting at the high school. A lot of them were standing on the front steps of Elston. Pretty good crowd," Hundt said. "There were a lot of cars running up and down Franklin. A lot of people on the sidewalks, whooping and hollering. They were celebrating!"

As the convoy of student buses made its way home and rumbled through the small towns of Indiana, people came out and waved, or honked their car horns at them. When they reached Michigan City, they couldn't believe the scene still unfolding.

It was nearing midnight, but "It was like it was the middle of the day," said cheerleader Nancy (Bobinski) White. "It was pretty hard to believe there were that many people up and that many lights on and people greeting us. People were everywhere—in the gym, out of the gym, in the parking lot—everywhere. And the gym was just jam-packed, even on the floor. We couldn't believe it."

Back in Indianapolis, the boys and their families celebrated at the Motor Inn. The hotel had an indoor pool on its roof and at 2:00 a.m., the staff told them they could have it to themselves, so the boys went swimming.

"*They* went swimming," Simmons pointed out. "I couldn't swim. Larry Gipson couldn't swim and we were on the side and Doug said, 'as good as you guys can play basketball, you mean to tell me that you can't swim?'"

Sunday morning, the press asked the players a few final questions while they ate their breakfast and little kids asked the boys for autographs. The team boarded their charter bus, took a lap around Memorial Circle monument in the center of Indianapolis, and then headed back to Michigan City.

Expecting another typical pep rally in Red Devil Gym, the boys were shocked at the scene that they witnessed. When they got twenty-seven miles from home, "There were people from LaCrosse all the way up Highway 421 yelling," said Cadwell. All along the highway at every pull-off, intersection, and vacant lot, cars sat with signs, fans waved, headlights flashed, and horns honked.

It was a beautiful spring day. The temperature touched sixty degrees. By noon, Franklin Street again choked with cars as people headed downtown to join the upcoming victory rally and to celebrate the state championship. Cars had new signs painted on their windows.

"STATE CHAMPS!"

"WE'RE #1."

"GO DEVILS GO!"

Red Devil pennants waved from car antennas. Signs in town had changed from "Hey, Hey! All the Way!" to "Hey, Hey! We WENT All the Way!"

The excitement, the enthusiasm, the energy—it was everywhere! The sidewalks jammed with people—dancing, laughing, cheering, and singing. Smiles, yes, the smiles! Everyone was smiling everywhere!

Dave Milcarek and a dozen friends had formed a snake line along the sidewalk, weaving through the crowd. When traffic stopped on the street, the head of the line opened the back passenger door of a large sedan, crawled through, opened the other back door and crawled out. The other twelve people in the line followed suit. Students' cars, adults' cars—it didn't matter. They did it again and again. Drivers laughed and traffic stood still until the snake line had completed its journey through the backseat.

When the team finally reached the city limits, they disembarked the bus and immediately were surrounded by a mob of people waving, cheering, and smiling. The cheerleaders met them and everyone climbed onto the ladder of a fire engine ladder truck.

"Now that was a shocker to me," Simmons said.

The fire engine proceeded not to Red Devil Gym, but the football stadium: Ames Field. All along the route people cheered and hollered. The boys couldn't believe it.

"We got to Ames Field, it was packed. Packed!" Simmons said.

"The bus barely made it through," said Morse. "We had to snake it through. Oh my God! How many people were there?"

A lot. One source estimated as many as 40,000 people turned out to greet the team and 12,000 people crowded into Ames Field for the victory rally.

During the seventy-five minute rally, the cheerleaders cheered, a banner was unveiled, a giant cake bearing multiple American flags was delivered, Warren Jones gave his battle cry:

Hey, hey, all the way!
Hey, hey, all the way!

One person after another paraded in front of the microphone to say a few words and fans wanted to hear from the players too.

"Everybody had to say something," said Morse. "That was *not* really cool. What were we going to say? After the first guy says it was a total team effort, it blows it for the other eleven guys."

What were they supposed to say?

Perhaps they should have talked about Brutal Ball. Told everybody about Fred LaBorn, Stanley Farmer, or Calvin George. Maybe mention that crowded ninth grade basketball game or getting to sweep the basketball court when they were in junior high. What it meant to be a Red Devil. They had the greatest fans. What it felt like to run through that iron hoop at a home game and hear the fans' yells. Maybe they should have talked about the up-and-overs, how much they believed in their coach and how much he really, truly loved them.

Would that have been too much? Would anybody have known what any of that meant? Their experiences—the fans and the players—were far different and yet it was all built around a shared geography, pride in their school, and a love of basketball. For the boys, it ended in Hinkle Fieldhouse. It was over. They had done what they set out to do: win. The fanfare surprised them. For the fans, it wasn't over. It meant something to them too. And they would ensure it lived on for years to come.

"People do remember and it is flattering. They talk about how that was the golden age of Michigan City, etcetera, and I am actually not jealous at all," said Rob McFarland. His daughter won a volleyball state championship for Michigan City High School in 1996. He'd love to see the high school win another state championship.

"I wish somebody else would win the state championship and bring it to town and do what we did. It would be great."

"They did get one," Simmons pointed out. "Marquette [Catholic High School] won [in 2014], but you know, they tried to discredit it as it wasn't the same with all this class A, B, etc. But they still won, though. It *was* a state championship."

"My wife says to this day, 'Don't you ever get enough of that?' I said, 'Not really. I can live with it.'" Morse said with a smile. "The whole thing was amazing building up to it, going through it, and the fifty years since then has been amazing because so many people still remember."

O'Neil, Cadwell, McFarland, Morse, Gipson, LaBorn, Krueger, Farmer, George, Kennedy, Adams, Garrett. They played as one. They stepped up when asked to do so, and sat down on the bench when they had to. They cheered on their teammates. They believed in one another. They trusted one another. They practiced hard together. They played together and worked together, down to the last player on the team.

There was no star player. None of them have been enshrined in the Indiana Basketball Hall of Fame. None of them ever will be. It's hard to win State. Fewer than ten percent of all Indiana high schools have won it. And it's rare for a team to win it all and not have a single member in the Hall of Fame.

Remember Jim Cadwell's words? They reflect the spirit of that team.

"We didn't really much care who scored, we just wanted to win."

Does your heart not sing when you read those words?

The men who played on that team are in their sixties today, but Al Whitlow still refers to them as "the kids." He paused to think about the kids, to try to describe them. A smile spread across his face and he leaned forward.

"They all had good senses of humor. Fun group of guys. Hard workers. I was really thrilled. It was a real pleasure to spend so much time with those guys. I had a lot of time with some of them." The tone in Whitlow's voice punctuated his sincerity.

The '66 Michigan City Elston Red Devils—a group of fun, selfless, hard-working, goofy kids.

A team through and through. One of the best.

Number one in Indiana in 1966.

How sweet it is, Al.

How sweet it is.

ACKNOWLEDGMENTS

Thank you to the following people who helped to make this book possible:

Shannon Miser-Carr (transcription)
James Robertson (cover design)
Al Whitlow
Warren Jones
Mike Adams
Terry Morse
Jim Cadwell
O'Neil Simmons
Rob McFarland
Dave Milcarek
Nancy (Bobinski) White
Roger & Nancy Bixler
Drew Tallackson (editor of *The Beacher*)

THE AUTHOR

Matt Werner grew up in Union Mills, Indiana. He earned degrees from Purdue University and Bowling Green State University. He is the author of the award-winning book,

SEASON OF UPSETS
Farm boys, city kids, Hoosier basketball
and the dawn of the 1950s

www.ingramcontent.com/pod-product-compliance
Lightning Source LLC
La Vergne TN
LVHW051808080426
835513LV00017B/1867